Saved for Real

Tonya Lee

Emerge Publishing Group, LLC
Riviera Beach, FL
www.emergepublishers.com

Library of Congress Control Number 2009939661

ISBN 978-0-9825699-1-7

Published by
Emerge Publishing Group, LLC
Riviera Beach, FL
www.emergepublishers.com

Tonya Lee, 2009
Saved for Real / Tonya Lee
1. Christianity. 2. Biographical.

Printed in the United States of America

Acknowledgements

Special Thanks To:

My Parents Charlie & Margaret Lee for being my first connection to the Lord by having me in church on a regular basis, even when I didn't want to go.

My friend Debbie Deloach for starting this good race to share my life story. You have been a Precious Stone for me to lean on.

My Spiritual parents Pastors Carnell & Ann Foster, for keeping me lifted in prayer and encouraging me to complete this task that the Lord has started.

My Family and other Friends who have been a part of sharing this experience with me, through their deeds, prayers, and their helping hands.

The Emerge Publishing group, and their editing team, in their great works to perfect and complete this book.

Contents

Dedication

I wish to dedicate this book to my Lord and Savior Jesus Christ, who watches over my spirit, soul, and body. Lord, you continue to send your grace and mercy every day of my life. I thank You for pressing upon my heart to share my story so that others may have a chance to come out of darkness like I did, so they too, may experience the marvelous light of your glory. Again I thank you, Jesus, A MILLION times over for saving me from the pit of HELL.

Foreword

During these perilous times, many may find themselves in bondages and caught in traps that the enemy has set to destroy precious souls. Even prior to deliverance, some of our sisters and brothers in Christ may have find themselves weighed down by the aftermath and consequences of falling into temptation. While for the believer, condemnation is not one of these consequences, a loss of faith is certainly a defeating purpose of sin. When our brethren are tied down in the traps of sin and bondage they are less effective at the great commission of "going out throughout the world and making disciples of all men." Christ promised us life, even an abundant life; that life begins at salvation; however, it is sometimes hindered by strongholds and snares derived by the enemy to affect our effectiveness in and for the Kingdom of GOD.

Tonya Lee was once caught in the vicious trap of homosexuality. The enemy was very proficient at luring and maintaining a hedge of deception over Lee for some number of years.

But our God, who is merciful and the definition of Grace, pursued Lee and delivered her from all unrighteousness by the Precious Blood of our Savior. This book is a testimony of God's goodness and grace. It is a testimony of how awesome God is at seeking the lost and delivering the bound.

In the book "Saved for Real", Lee takes us through her process of being set free. She pours out her heart to all those who have ears to hear. Her transparency is a blessing as she walks in her calling to draw others into the marvelous light of our Savior. And while her struggles were mostly in the areas of overcoming sexual sin, her testimony is good news for anyone who is struggling in any areas as all have sinned and fallen short of the glory of God. Her story resounds with the hope of our God as our Deliverer.

The enemy's intentions were to sift Lee as wheat, but now that she has been converted, she is a testament of God's love, mercy, power and grace. As you read this epistle of deliverance and her pursuit of God, I pray that your heart will be good ground to receive the abundance of His grace through her story. *"Finally, beloved I wish above all things that you may prosper and be in health even as your soul prospers."* 3 John 2

Forgetting those things which are behind and reaching forth unto these things which are before and pressing toward the mark for the prize of the high calling of God in Christ Jesus (Philippians 3:13-14).

-Thonda Ollis-Bellamy

XII

Introduction

This book is a true testimony of my life from the beginning to the present time. I was not always "Saved". I went to church on a regular basis as a young girl, a teenager, and young adult, also into my late 30's and 40's. Finally, I got **"Saved for Real"**.

The title of this book came about after I had an encounter, or shall I say a meeting in my living room with Jesus. This took place just prior to Easter Sunday 2003.

This book, "Saved For Real", is a true testimony of my life. It shares what my Heavenly Father has begun and continues to do in my life. It is my hope and prayer that my story will be a blessing and help to others who desire to be set free from bondage, curses, and generational curses such as lesbianism/homosexuality, drugs, alcoholism, gambling, and any other forms of darkness.

The Lord is calling for all to be delivered, healed, and set free from all afflictions. Please open your mind, heart and soul to our Lord. Surrender your life to him and trust him. He will do what He says He will do. As you read the pages of my heart (this Book) and as you seek the Lord and His righteousness, He promises everything else will be added unto you. Each testimony that you will read shows a level of growth in Christ. Jesus says "If you seek me, you will find me, If you knock the door shall be open unto you, Ask it will be given unto You". My sisters and brothers, make sure you're asking according to His will, not yours.

Remember, He's the creator not you. He loves you and will never stop loving you.

He's still seeking for all of his sheep to come unto him. Jesus said *"If you abide in me, I will in turn abide in you"*. Our God is high above on the throne, looking to and fro, seeking after those who have their hearts steadfast on him, so he may show himself mighty on their behalf. He's waiting. Come, will you join me in serving him? I ask again that you open your hearts and learn from my story, something that may be able to help you or someone else.

GOD BLESS YOU!

Chapter 1

Who Was I Then

On Saturday, August 15th, 1956 approximately 2:45pm in the west wing of Miami's infamous Jackson Memorial Hospital, the youngest of five children was born to Margaret and Charlie: Tonya Yvette Lee.

I would learn later from my parents, that we initially resided in Perrine, the southwest area of Miami. Little did I know, I'd return to this area as an adult and purchase my first home. Little did I know, I would live in Green Hill Estates for several years, before turning it over to my partner, companion and lover of thirteen years. But that's another story.

Allow me to cover the basics and family, first.

Margaret and Charlie Lee were my parents whom I loved dearly. The parents who I cherished, honored, fought for and protected, also gave birth to four other children before my arrival. That doesn't matter when you're last. Yes, I'm "The baby". And although I preferred being called 'the youngest', in private mom would always remind me that I was the baby, her "baby." In fact, she said this up until the day she was called home.

I still long to hear her voice sometimes. I'm writing this chapter and it's only been eight months since she's been gone. I'll probably never stop missing mom; but I'm confident, I'll see her again.

In the beginning my dad, Charles Sr., the second of three children, was born to Gertrude and Willie Lee. I remember him being a good looking, quiet man, with a big heart. Well, at least I thought he was, and apparently my mom did too. Even when he aged, and got the 'old man spread', I still saw him as my handsome hero. He was truly a great man in my eyes. A real man, I might add. I obviously still have high concepts about Daddy, because I'm picturing him and smiling.

Before I was born, he had already worked twenty-five years for one particular company. He bought his paychecks home and made sure there was food on the table, rent paid, clothes on our backs and shoes on our feet. What a provider he was!

In January, 1982 at the young age of fifty-four, my Father and hero went home. Way too soon, I thought. My parents had been married for thirty-four years before his untimely death and my mother never married again. My mom was also a special lady. When I was old enough to attend kindergarten, my mom began working full time to help cover the expenses of sending five children to school.

Mom, like me, was also spoiled rotten to the core. Her maiden name was McQueen. She was the seventh and last child born to Henry and Hattie McQueen. Grandma had six boys, and yes, mom was also the baby.

As I write and think back now, I remember mom always being such a lady. I must put emphasis on her being lady-like because with so many boys and brothers in the house, there's usually aggressiveness in the girl. Not so with mom. I never detected any 'tom-boyish' habits or tendencies in her demeanor. I suppose it's safe to say that Grandma Hattie wasn't having it! (smile). She said Grandma taught her how to cook and keep a clean house, in order to prepare her for marriage. And I can attest to the tasty meals and cleanliness that my Grandmother, Ms. Hattie McQueen, taught mom very well. Thanks Grandma!

On August 1st, 1949 in Miami, Florida, my parents wed. Born to this union were the five I mentioned before. In 1950, the first born was Charlie, Jr. (named after Daddy). In 1951, the second birth was given to Henry. The third born was another boy, James, 1953. In 1955, Cynthia, the first girl was born.

Saving the fifth and best for last, is Tonya. I'm writing and I'm smiling, of course. I've learned to balance being 'the baby' and sometimes, the most responsible over the years, without being heady. But today, God is teaching me to balance a whole new thing; even how to be corrected. It is partly my parents fault for spoiling and not disciplining me. (There it goes again, my old fault finding spirit). That brings me to the subject of dysfunction. I grew up in an environment saturated with it.

Growing Up

The saying goes, when you know better, you automatically should do better. Right? Wrong.

That's not always the case. Truth is, you must have a made up mind to want to do right or better than what you've experienced in life.

Over the years, I experienced things that I knew in my heart were wrong or that there was something 'right' missing. I knew that families weren't supposed to do what my family was always doing. I remember the parties almost every other month for all types of occasions: graduations, marriages, birthdays, anniversaries and funerals. We either had them at our house, or close friends and other families' houses. This also gave reason and excuse to drinking.

After a while, you just knew what to expect on the weekends. You also knew wherever there was drinking, arguments and fights would follow. Yes, you heard right, fights! Verbal assaults and physical altercations between families! We (the kids) would actually be placed on the outside of the apartment, while mom and dad argued and fought.

On several occasions, we were in the midst of the fights, throwing shoes and pots at my dad to get him off and keep him off my mom. Boy! Talk about dysfunctional! I grew up watching a provider and a home maker fight like enemies sometimes. Dad would literally lock all of us outside (to include my mom) until he decided to let us back in.   And sometimes, that would be the next morning.

We would have to sleep down the street at Grandma's house; and sometimes at my god-sisters apartment.   This was embarrassing, of course. Eventually, the entire neighborhood knew to look for the 'Lee family side show' at least twice a month.

At age eight I developed asthma due to stress; and it was activated whenever my parents argued and fought. I also learned to use this ailment (this spirit of affliction) to my advantage. You see, my father was also a compassionate man. I loved him for that, even in his dysfunction.

When they discovered I was asthmatic, Dad stopped putting me outside with the rest of the family. This was to my advantage because it became my way to help protect my mom and brothers from constant embarrassment. I would wait until dad was fast asleep from his drunken stupor, and then let the others back inside the apartment.

We're talking about a two bedroom apartment. My parents took the first bedroom for themselves. The second bedroom was ours, five kids. Cynthia and I shared a king size bed. Henry and Charlie also shared a king size bed, and James slept alone in a single bed. No doubt we had the largest of the two rooms; and to think that we were living large! Ha! As large as my little mind thought we were. And even though we had to deal with daily dysfunctions, I still felt special because (unlike many black fathers) Dad lived with us and took very good care of the household. No doubt our shelter, our car and our clothes were a big plus in the neighborhood.

Now as for church, we attended service on the first and third Sunday of every month. These were special dates because my mother ushered or was part of the special programs being held. Sunday started a normal week of peace for us, and Thursday ended it. Friday, could surely be counted on for 'no peace' in the house. It never failed.

After years of fighting, my mother resorted to the kitchen for knives to defend herself against my father; but dad would always end up taking the knife from her. There was one incident where my mom actually stabbed my dad with a barbeque fork. I recall the blood coming from his chest. Frantic and yelling all over the place for someone to call an ambulance, I ran across the street to my grandparent's house and screamed that mom had just killed dad! What else is an eleven year old supposed to do after seeing that much blood? What did I know then? Not too much, right? I only knew I didn't want my dad to die, and thanks be to God he didn't.

Shortly after this one incident which put so much fear in my mom, the drama of the physical fights came to a complete halt, yet there was still the continual drinking and arguments of old. Unfortunately, we not only grew up with this, we actually grew quite used to it.

This now brings me to the dysfunctional relations we all had with each other. Words to the wise: "Don't compare your children to each other; it's not healthy." It causes sibling rivalries. Sure, my mother made certain we were well taken care of, even if it meant denying my father and herself. But there were still mind games and comparisons. Today, I see how it affected us in the end. This is probably why Cynthia and I have never been close. We all love each other, of course. We really don't have a choice. But truth be told, we've led different lives and lifestyles which ultimately kept us all distant.

I remember my brothers being much closer with each other than Cynthia and I. I admired them so much growing up. They protected me knowing I was the terror in our neighborhood. I was determined to have my way and usually started a fight to prove it. If I didn't win, I would summon my sister to fight for me against the kids I couldn't beat. Thanks to Cynthia who finished every incident I started; she would fight until I called on our brothers, who responded each and every time, as my heroes.

Growing Pains

Both my eldest brothers entered the U.S armed forces. The oldest, Charlie, enlisted in the Air force at age eighteen. The second oldest, Henry, enlisted in the army. Charlie, after three years into his tour of duty was given an honorable discharge and 100% disability.

Since then, my brother has never been the same. There was something going on in him beyond the dysfunction we endured as children. Once home. Charlie no longer looked like the brother I once knew nor did he act normal.

We would soon discover that his disability was mental. Charlie was diagnosed as being Paranoid Schizophrenic. At first, it sounded like a brain-wash job to me. I blamed the army for sending my brother back home with these trained abnormalities, but where did the initial dysfunctions really come from? On the other hand, Henry completed his four year tour of duty but would return home to a week of tragedy. None of us expected this life time of pain, nor did we expect the 'curse' of dysfunction to run it's course.

Before enlisting in the Military, Charlie bought a home, got married and had one son, Calvin. Shortly after his return, neither lived with him because of the unpredictable physical and mental abuse; in addition to the psych medications he was prescribed. Charlie would go into these fits of rage and jealousy accusations.

His wife, enduring as much as she could, escaped with my nephew, and filed for divorce. I thank God for keeping them through that time; especially since none of us knew that Charlie's mental condition was capable of making him a murderer. There's nothing deadlier than alcohol consumption and psych medications; and I do mean deadly!

The Unforgettable Night

James, my youngest brother, had moved to Sarasota to live with his girlfriend and eighteen month old son. James would also come back and forth to visit the family. Once while here in town,

James borrowed Charlie's car to go and put in an application at Miami Dade Community College for the upcoming fall term. James had made up his mind to transition back to Miami and go to school again. My other brother, Henry, was also interested in furthering his education and went also.

Meanwhile, Charlie, who thought James was taking way too long with his car, went into a rage of anger. When James finally arrived (by nightfall) Charlie's physical attack on him cost him his life. James was stabbed in the heart multiple times by Charlie.

The end result of this case and findings was Charlie's incompetence to stand trial, by excusable means of insanity. He would be housed at south Florida State Hospital for three years, in the psych ward. I personally disowned and disliked my brother after causing the family such pain and sorrow. It took many, many years for me to forgive him, but I eventually did, and God gets the Glory.

Henry, my second oldest brother had only been home a few days after being discharged from the army. He and his girlfriend would return the next morning from an evening of fun to a tragedy. When Mom, Dad and I arrived at Charlie's house, James, my youngest brother, lay dead under a tree.

Charlie, had been detained in the back of a squad car where he continued to yell and kick the glass in full rage. I was nineteen at the time. I didn't have a personal relationship with the Lord back then, but I remember crying out to Him for help. I was so hurt. The pain was so deep then.

Even now that I'm in Covenant (and it seems easier to re-visit this area), I still need the strength and mighty power of God to keep me in constant forgiveness.

The Unforgettable Scene

I'll never forget it. James was covered. Mom was crying, yelling and screaming, "No, no, not my son!" The paramedics had a monitor on Dad's chest; He was in anguish and not breathing well. And there I stood, not knowing what to do, but stand there. I tried convincing myself to move, to react, to do something! Wanting so bad to help, I ended up crying aloud with my Mom.

At the same time, I was sisterly concerned about Charlie and Henry. Where was he? Where could he be, while this is happening to us? Did he even know yet? Seconds later Cynthia arrived with her husband and daughter, asking "What's going on? What's happened?" Where's Charlie? Where's James? The next day, Henry arrived at Charlie's house and witnessed the Police Security Tape still tied to the tree outside. He would miss the horrific scene of James having been killed in cold blood.

Moments after the incident, we begin to question ourselves. What if? Maybe I should've? Perhaps, I could've? If I'd been there this never would have happened." Henry made these statements continuously, as if his presence would've prevented the situation. These "family to the rescue" symptoms and arguments would plague us for days to come, weeks to come, month's, perhaps, years.

Everyone was having a personal pity-party. Then came "the blame-game" syndrome. My Mom, still in denial, said that someone else did it. Someone else killed James. My Dad, quiet and unmoved by anything, anymore, turned to drinking heavier on weekends. My sister Cynthia stayed away for a while.

The only good that came from this incident was my parents being granted custody of James's son, Jermaine, for a few years, by permission of his girlfriend. My nephew bought a temporal comfort. He was the missing part of us, missing James. We all grew attached to Jermaine and then the inevitable happened. His mom came (due to social security benefits) and picked him up for good.

Chapter 2

Life, Experiences: Adolescent Years

A llow me to back up a little between the ages of thirteen and fifteen. It was the hardest, roughest, or should I just say most "vulnerable" time of my life. (Parents, be especially aware of these years). All my heroes/brothers had left home. Cynthia was dating and soon to be married. No one was there anymore to watch and govern my every move like my siblings did.

At fourteen, with Mom's approval, I started my first summer job. It was a good thing. It was like I had my very own responsibility - because I had my own money.   I also had my own direction and started smoking marijuana. I started popping pills, Red devils and Quaaludes. The devil took a hold of me, early on. Satan made sure I had access to any drug I wanted or needed. Access was right there in the neighborhood where I lived and laughed, and got high with my friends.

Parents, beware. Invite your children's friends over; communicate openly with them. Know with whom they're socializing and keeping company. Or you'll never know, like my parents didn't, that I was doing cocaine. Yes, I said it, Cocaine. I used to smoke it in my cigarettes; back then it was called "geeking or lacing." This was before they started smoking it from a pipe and calling it crack.

My Mom and Dad never knew it, though. In fact, they gave me permission to smoke cigarettes at age 16; as long as I was able to purchase my own habit. Little did they know I was already stealing cigarettes from my Dad's pack two years before. I also tried drinking heavy liquor. No thanks! I couldn't get past the burning sensation in my throat and stomach. I figured I had enough addictive issues with smoking and the other drugs. I never realized how many issues I had at that time.

At age fifteen I began working at Miami's infamous burger shop, Royal Castle. I lied about my age and told Pete, the manager, I was seventeen with a two-year old son, named Calvin, who was really Charlie's son. I felt so attached to my nephew that it made the lie seem okay. Besides that, this was my first real job. The manager was respectful and cool. This made working for him even better.

Being employed allowed me to give Mom about fifty dollars a month. It also provided me the money to fund my habits. I began socializing with everyone in the neighborhood that did my choice of drugs. Slowly, but surely, the drugs began to effect my entire life. My entire way of thinking and doing things had changed. I began working part-time on the weekends, so church was like totally out of the picture. My thoughts regarding Sunday service was, "Later for that!"

By the time I turned sixteen, I was coming in my parent's house whatever time of night I felt like it; particularly on the weekends. Remember, Mom and Dad didn't get drunk during the week. The joke amongst ourselves was that they were 'weekend alcoholics'. Anyway, while my addiction for drugs grew, so did my appetite to try drinking again. Wine coolers and beer became my choices for an extra buzz. I was no longer interested in going to school. As a matter of fact, my tenth and eleventh grade years were hell. That's exactly what it was, a living hell! But I did it to myself.

For a year and a half, I was transferred back and forth from Miami Northwestern to Miami Edison and then Miami Central Senior High. There was always something wrong with the schools, the teachers or the students; never me. I played the blame game quite well with my parents. Rightfully so; I learned it from them. No school was right for me; I concluded that it was a waste of time, so I quit going.

I had no responsibilities other than buying my clothes and of course, my drugs. Things began to crumble around me. To keep from appearing to be a drop-out, I would get up, get dressed and pretend to go to school. Finding drug holes to pill pop, lace-up and drink was really what I aimed to do, all day. Every day.

After months and months of this destructive behavior, I ended up being rushed to the Hospital. Yes, it's back to Jackson Memorial Hospital. All of my vital signs were taken and blood was drawn for testing. I knew my parents would soon find out that their precious "baby girl" was using drugs. I was the one they had the most confidence in, the one most likely to make it to college, the one they proclaimed being most responsible and obedient to whatever they said.

Perhaps, I was seeking their attention. Perhaps I needed more than just their permission and approval. I believe each child needs this in a certain measure from their parents; but it should be fused with love and concern.

My Mom sat in the emergency room with me. Only God knows what was going through her mind. When the test results came back it devastated them. At first no one could believe it. I saw the confusion, hurt and disappointment in their faces. They also informed my Mom that I was no longer a virgin, which she would question me about later.....

Parents, please be wise. Talk to your children about sex. Advise them how important it is to refrain from intercourse. Teach them how and why to save themselves for marriage. I told Mom the truth. I lost my virginity at fourteen. I didn't have an ongoing relationship with this boy. I was just curious. I never had sex again until I was sixteen. It just did not seem right. It didn't feel right, or was my interest leading me to something else? Keep reading. You'll understand later.

I thank God for being the God of second chances. During this period of puberty, I was told by

my Mother, "Don't bring no babies in my house!"
My interpretation of mom's scolding was, "You can
have sex, but don't have any babies!" Well, truth is
I was never interested in having a baby, anyway. I
didn't want to raise a child in the same
dysfunctional environment that I grew up in.

My pledge to do right, and be right came in the
crying out to my parents for us to move out of the
neighborhood. "Sugar Hill." It should've been
called "Sugar Hell." It was one of many holes in
Liberty City: a ghetto set up by the enemy to kill
dreams and people with vision; a place full of poison
and corruption; a place to promote drugs and street
hustle; a place of wrong influence, and exposure; a
place for cell-mates and prison sentences and a
bottom-less pit to prostitute and destroy lives.

In august of 1973 several months after my plea,
we moved to Carol City and bought our first
home. We were starting over in a new house
and most importantly, with new people in a
new neighborhood.

Even after the embarrassment of my drug habit
and non-attendance in school, my parents seemed
to still have such a confidence in me to do better.
And I did! I felt encouragement and began to excel

in all my studies. My intentions were to graduate on time and with my class in June, 1974.

I was eager to prove to myself and my parents that their sacrifice was not in vain. I would attend all my classes to include the night school courses four times a week. I was three credits behind and needed to make up the lost time. I graduated in August 1974, two-months later than expected, but I still received my diploma.

My First Milestone

I became totally focused on nothing else but school. I made up my mind; no more drugs, no more drinking, no more hanging out, and for now no more employment, just school! After graduating I attended a First Aid class and became certified as a Nurses' Aid. I enjoyed this position and wanted to continue my interest in nursing. So I enrolled into Miami-Dade Junior College, and received a two-year Basic Education Opportunity Grant (BEOG). This was considered free money for college. This also afforded me the position as a part-time student assistant with compensation every two weeks. I figure it was a good enough salary for an eighteen year old still living at home.

I began my two-year journey at MDCC in 1975 and received an Associate of Arts Degree. I truly enjoyed school. I met many people and made many acquaintances, but I still had no interest in dating, whatsoever.

My greatest desire (and still is) was to complete college. My routine was school, studies, the assistant part-time job and if I felt like it, a once a month Friday or Saturday outing. I learned to drive and was allowed to take my parents to the usual weekend parties with family and friends. I insisted on being the personal chauffeur for mom and dad because of their heavy drinking. After all I put them through, I believed I was responsible for protecting them.

As I write this portion of the book, I'm thinking back to some of the episodes when I had to wake them after the party and friends would help me get them to the car. However, when we arrived home, I was the only one to physically man them both. With no other assistance. Boy! Talk about methods of maneuvering! From hot packs to cold packs, to buckets of H2o! Whatever it took to wake them and move them, from the car to the house, hey, I did it! Yes, I can actually laugh about it today, but that was incredibly hard on a teenager. A female at that!

Because they were both working class, church-going people, my parents always denied being alcoholics. And who was I to argue with them? What's the 'Baby' girl to do but keep on loving and protecting them? It was only the three of us at home. Everyone else had grown-up, gone off and made their own nest.

Watching my parents go from responsible tax payers, to irresponsible drunkards, made me vow not to ever again place myself in a position where I wasn't in control. I vowed it over every aspect of my life. This big ambition of mine was short lived all because of the word, "love." Or should I say, what you think is love. When you think you're in it, no one in the world can tell you any different.

Real love or real lust?

My first love, or so I thought was "Mr. Danny." I met him at Miami Dade Community College (M.D.C.C.) He approached me and if I remember correctly, he stated that we attended a class together. He introduced himself as a gentleman and I returned the lady-like favor, with pleasure. With little or no experience with men, I thought he seemed quite the polite type. We engaged in conversation for about one hour, and afterwards, he asked for my phone number. It was an even exchange.

I walked away thinking that he was smooth with words and quick with answers. He may be a manipulator, perhaps, a city slicker. But it didn't matter, because I vowed to be in control, remember? So when he called we talked and talked and talked and then we mutually decided to date. (Wise Words: In the event of a distraction, stay plugged in to your heart's desire). I had no intention of dating anybody until I had completed my first four years of college. Wow! What a distraction! What a dramatic turn of events I involved myself in.

Chapter 3

The Roller Coaster

This is exactly the type of involvement Mr. Danny and I had. I didn't care because I was in love.... excuse me, in lust. This man appeared to be between twenty-one and twenty-three. After four months of dating, I would discover that he was actually thirteen years my senior. Yes, go ahead and count it up. I was eighteen years old and Mr. Danny was thirty-one. He also revealed that he was divorced, and was raising two sons from his previous marriage. He not only attended school, but worked full-time as a computer operator for the City of Miami Police Department. He owned his own home and appeared to be financially stable. A teenager would find that admirable, right? So I admired him and I ended up loving him. (Oh, let's be real!) I was in lust with him and full of lust for him.

I tell you, I didn't care how he treated me or what else he did as long as he sexed me. I reserved my weekends (every one of them) just for that. (In order to help you I must be transparent here). Six months into this lust-filled rollercoaster of ours, there was this one weekend I couldn't go over to his house. Needless to say, I was pissed off to the highest! I decided to stay away from Mr. Danny for approximately six months. I called this period my coasting down time.

Mr. Danny persuaded me, of course, to come over and see him. Convinced that he missed me, I fell right back into the sex-trap again. Six-months on, six months off. Six months here, six months there. Why couldn't he keep a committed pattern with me? Why was he so busy and secretive all the time? It aggravated me. No, I didn't like it. But I didn't care, either. As long as I had his sex, I was satisfied.

A year and a half later, Mr. Danny would confide in me a secret he kept since day one of his meeting me. Mr. Danny, all this time, was bisexual. You can't imagine the stage of shock I was in after hearing how he toyed with my life and my affections.

Knowing the dangers of this sick cycle, you would think I ended the drama right then. No. I remained in lust. I was in a reprobate state of mind and didn't even know it. I actually believed I was in control and was able to change him.

A T T E N T I O N: RED FLAG!!!! My sisters and my brothers you are NOT capable of changing anyone's desires. That change has to come from within them! My advice is that you run for your very L I F E!!!!! Ha! But did I run? No. I thought I had all Mr. Danny needed in these hips!

Listen to me, carefully. It doesn't matter how masculine built or how fine and shapely you think you are. I'm smiling as I write this segment. I can tell you straight-up about the drag-queens, those female impersonators out there, that your so-called real man is secretly seeing and calling. Yeah. Your man of steel. Your man of thunder. The down-low brother. Like mine, Mr. Danny. I didn't have to have any evidence. I didn't have to look for signs. The man just came flat-out and told me, and I still couldn't be true to myself. Just like some of you.

Sure I knew that a duck was a duck. I know how a duck is supposed to look. I know how a duck is supposed to waddle when it walks, and I know how a duck is supposed to sound when it quacks, but I had a swan and I knew it. I just refused to pull my hard-head out of the sand and open my eyes. Somebody help me, is right!

Okay, now it's two years later. Mr. Danny is taking me to Gay and Lesbian Clubs and Lounges all over town. It dawned on me later that he was dropping phone numbers and picking up men. My God. Talk about being caught-up in bondage. I had developed so much lust for this man that I still thought he would change and be all mine, one day. That kept me waiting and wanting more and more attention from him. I began doing whatever he did. Just to be around him. Just to be with him, just to be one of his. (A T T E N T I O N: Brothers and sisters: Ungodly spirits are transferable).

Now let me continue and tell you the whole truth of the matter. Eventually, I got used to these clubs. I'd give out my phone number and accept a few as well. I also danced with different girls, dirty dancing. At that time it really didn't mean anything. Remember, I was only there because of Mr. Danny. My thoughts were on him the entire time. I anticipated going home with my man to get a full night of satisfaction. Boy, was I plumb dumb! I wasn't aware that we were also taking those same spirits of perversion home to the bed, with us!

Three years later, I was still in school and still in sex. Noticed I said sex, not love. Anyway, in 1977 we both graduated from Miami-Dade and were now attending Florida International University. We both decided to stay in the field of social work. I attended school three days a week and was hired at South Florida State Hospital, midnight shift.

We're talking a full load of responsibility here; but I was still high from the excitement of keeping my word and graduating, so it was cool. I was now twenty-one years of age. My parents were quick to remind me, "You're not grown until you're able to house, clothe and feed yourself!" I was also reprimanded by them and told that staying out all night was no longer acceptable. This statement insinuated that they knew Mr. Danny and I were physically involved.

Yet the rule of the day still stood: *"Don't bring no babies in this house that you can't take care of completely!"* In other words, have all the sex you want, but don't get pregnant, Tonya.

But I did get pregnant by this man that I lusted after, and I really wanted this baby. Mr. Danny had different plans, though. After finding out, he immediately began to talk about an abortion. He reminded me of how important finishing school was; and that I only had a year to go. Dumb me. I began to second guess and question myself. Do I really need a baby, at twenty-two years of age? What about my parent's rule? I couldn't possibly go to work and school full-time.

Then came the rude awakening from Mr. Danny. I'll never forget it. He said "I can't take care of any more children! Whoa! No need to think about it anymore. Believe it or not, remembering those words he said still hurts a little. So, I aborted the fetus. It took many years after that to forgive myself. Willingly taking an innocent life is an act of murder; and I did it. But God was in the forgiving business back then and he still is now.

The year is 1980. I was still riding the rollercoaster with Mr. Danny. But something was changing; I just didn't know what. Prior to graduating, I begin to feel differently about him. He no longer appealed to me. He couldn't talk me into having sex as often as we used to. His smooth words were now constant reminders of how easy he talked me into having an abortion. It's like the subconscious bulb in my head got brighter and brighter. In my heart I harbored resentment towards him for not wanting our baby. I was angry at him for not having the same feelings that I did about our child. I was also angry at myself.

Nothing was the same; not even the lustful drive that once so easily beset me. Then he decided to make matters worse: he suggested a threesome. That threesome with me, him and another female sex partner never occurred. However, the suggestion alone did initiate my involvements with women. In fact, the same female he introduced me to was the one I had my first lesbian encounter with.

This one experience triggered and loosed the transferable spirits of homosexuality. Every other lover that Mr. Danny had (outside of me) was now a part of me; body and soul. I was still satisfied with Mr. Danny, but I craved with lust for something else. I wanted more of whatever it was that triggered me.

The one night stands with women began. I didn't have relationships with them, just encounters. Nothing serious. Well, not yet anyway. Mind you, I'm still living at home with my parents. But nobody suspects me of anything other than being with Mr. Danny; and that involvement was more distant than ever, and dangling by very short threads.

The year was still 1980. Going to funerals was sort of like a past-time hobby for my mom. If she knew you or remembered you, mom was going. Sure I thought it was strange; but hey, that was her thing. Well, one evening she asked me to escort her to a wake. I didn't have any plans and the person who passed was actually from the old neighborhood. Satan was behind this too. I just didn't know it at that time.

The elderly woman who passed away was Karen's Grandmother. When we were kids I remember both Karen and her mom being the neighborhood lesbians. Everybody knew it. And now all grown up, I revealed that I too, had women "F R I E N D S". The word "FRIEND" is a label amongst the Gay population. So began our involvement.

Karen, the same neighbor that watched me grow up, would undoubtedly become my first female lover for the next nine months. That was yet another lust filled rollercoaster ride that ended abruptly when she crashed my automobile. Karen, whom I trusted to use my car while I was at work, was supposed to pick me up at work. Boy, would I walk outside to a surprise that evening. When she returned to my job, my car had been involved in an accident. Karen told me she ran into my co-worker's car right there in the parking lot.

In addition to listening to this bizarre story of how it happened, I also noticed that her speech was slurred. She seemed different. She was unusually quiet and almost incoherent. I watched her behavior patterns and I knew something was wrong, probably because I identified with these same patterns in my past. An investigation revealed that she had been drinking and using drugs, cocaine in particular. I had already been through enough with drug abuse in my past and I didn't need it, or her anywhere in my future

In addition to that I was now employed by the Department of Probation and Parole. I was only twenty-three, but I had some experience under my belt and a little common sense. Karen would never drive my car, again. I never saw her again either. I was also very grateful that my co-worker didn't press any charges. Whew! I needed a break!

For the next six months, I didn't want to be involved with anyone, anywhere, at anytime, especially when you've been marked by Satan.

While working for Probation, a co-worker approached me to share her experience with me about a party she attended. At least that's what I thought she was doing. Later during the discussion she informed me that 'I' also, was at this particular party and she had the pictures to prove it. "Okay, so prove it", I said. The following day, she did exactly that. During lunch we engaged in open-ended conversations about our past and our lifestyle.

At first we were just lesbian friends and then three months later, we were lovers. Yes, once again I became involved in lust. However, this one wasn't short lived. Since day one of our conversing at work, this one would be different from the others. This one had its own pre-planned route. This one would be the first to take on the term, 'relationship' This one was birthed from a discourse of influence (meaning both our experiences) - and lasted for a period of thirteen solid years.

We were compatible in many ways. We had both been hurt by men, and felt they could no longer be trusted. We were around the same age. We both shared the same values and goals. We had professional jobs, with lucrative pay scales that allowed us to travel wherever we desired. We both showered each other during holidays and birthdays with love gifts and made everything seem so real, so special, so right. We even purchased our first home as a married couple.   You heard right, I said married.

There was only one thing that she had and I didn't. She already had a man in her life, a kind, beautiful, and very respectful six-year old man, I'll call Keith. I grew so attached to him that I claimed him as my own. I loved Keith with the love of a mother because I remember so desperately wanting to be one. So, I took advantage of this opportunity. I became his legal guardian and second mom. And we all lived as one big happy family; because we had each other, because it seemed right.

The terms or the differences didn't matter to me. In my mind, I was living large, very large, and very wrong. Thank God, Keith grew up to become a fine young man. At nineteen years of age, he enlisted in the U.S. Navy, and was excited about leaving. Keith never spoke about it, but perhaps he secretly wanted to get away from our beautiful yet, "immoral" home; away from our fabricated parenthood, and the lesbian lifestyle he literally had to accept as a child.

Only the Lord knows what he grew up thinking, or what he may have shared with his friends. We never forced him to believe in what we did or how we lived. I don't care how well a kid is bred and instructed. I would never agree to homosexuals adopting, even if I weren't Christian. It's just not a wholesome environment for children, period. I Thank God that he didn't end up angry or hating us. I Thank God that Keith was neither tainted nor influenced by our choice.

I'd like to acknowledge God's grace and mercy even now. And Father, I thank you for hearing the many cries of those who were in constant prayer for our very souls. Amen.

Pride, Rebellion and Whoredom

During this lifestyle, I vowed the "act of marriage" twice. (Listen honey - AnyBODY can get married - just like anybody can act). I should know. We were married after the first three years into this relationship; and then we re-dedicated our vows after ten years. Why? Uh.....because I was whorish, that's why. As if renewing vows to a woman would make a difference to God. As if allowing a homosexual to conduct both ceremonies would be acceptable in His sight. Please. I needed to be renewed by the transformation of my mind, first. But I didn't want that. I wanted my way. I wanted to be slick and smooth and cunning like Mr. Danny taught me or should I say, double-minded like Mr. Danny's doubled and troubled lifestyle.

This is one of many results when spirits transfer. It leads to a wide road of constantly needing to be satisfied in your flesh. Most times, by more than one person.

The woman that I twice married was the love of my life or so I thought. In my reprobate mind and heart I believed there would never be another. I gave my all and shared my all with her. No one knew me or ever got to know me like she did. That was long before I found out about having the "No Greater Love" than this from the Lord of Lords.

What is the spirit of pride?

Pride is the very foundation upon which satan has built his kingdom. This spirit's origin finds its way into the very heart of satan. In a way it can be said that satan himself spawned this spirit. Pride is an inflated perception of ones own dignity and self worth. When pride manifests itself it often manifests as arrogance disdainful conduct or treatment, haughtiness or even false humility. Pride is a protector of "self". It does not betray self, expose self or tell on self. It is obsessed with self. Pride goeth before destruction and a haughty spirit before a fall." Proverbs 16:18. Thank you Jesus for your healing deliverance and setting free power upon my life and for each one who chose to partake of your promises. There are many signs, symptoms and manifestations of the spirit of pride. I will disclose on a few to make my point. Pride displays itself in haughtiness, rebellion, wrath, defensiveness, conceit, disobedience, independence, self-importance, vanity egotism, uncontrolled anger and resentment. I, myself once portrayed all these. But GOD!!!

Now! The Spirit of Rebellion: Works well with the spirit of pride, this spirit resists government and authority in all forms. It drives it's hosts to blatantly or passively disobey. It is non-compliant to protocol, order or ordinances. The Word of God says, " for rebellion is as the sin of witchcraft, and stubbornness is as iniquity and adultery. Because thou hast rejected the word of the Lord, he has also rejected thee from being King." (I Samuel 15:23 NKJV). We must pray for our Lord to release true humility, submission, repentance and the Love of God in our hearts. [1]

Chapter 4

Deliverance Begins Here

Prior to giving my first testimony, it had been approximately one and a half years living totally in Christ. I was so hungry for anything that would be fulfilling to my Spirit man: books, CDs, and Videos. I was becoming a brand-new creature II Corinthians 5:17 NKIV) *"Therefore, if anyone is in Christ, he is a new creation; old things have passed away; behold, all things have become new."* I was being transformed. My spirit was eager to please God.

My greatest hobby is reading. The books I used to read, I removed them from my home and replaced them with spiritual books, powerful books.

Well, just to name a few: Good Morning Holy Spirit, The God Chasers, Fruit of the Spirits, Daughter of Destiny, Divine Revelation of Heaven, The Power of the Blood, Vessel of Honor, Secrets of the Vine, and The Prayer of Jabez.

Most of my rap was replaced with gospels, and some jazz. I replaced all of my radio stations and plugged in what was going to increase me totally. I was never that big on television personally. But, I also changed my program to a station that was going to enhance my spirit and soul-man. And yes, I had to change friends and associates. Many things from the past cannot come with you to the future. My entire wardrobe was replaced as well.

A few of the many people I associated with were considered close friends. Yes, I still love them and pray for them often but my relationship with Jesus outweighs any friendship with any man. Jesus said, *"For whoever does the will of God is my brother, and my sister and mother."* (Mark 3:35) Some may even be thinking that I'm being a little frantic. Well, I tell you like this; it took drastic measures to bring me out of that lifestyle with that "sprit of perversion". It was not easy but I believe all things are possible with God. Only He can bring you all the way out. We have been given a way of escape from every trial, tribulation, and temptation.

My Testimony- August 22nd, 2004

Greetings to each of you. I don't come to you with eloquent speech, but to share with you "God's Amazing Grace" upon my life. Two weeks before Easter Sunday, I entered the Pembroke Pines Church 2003 due to a flyer I received in the mail. I was in search of a new home to serve my Lord. I had just a couple weeks before been set free from a Lifestyle of Homosexuality of 23 years.

Satan had me bound with this stronghold for many years, but to God I give all the Glory. He gave me the best gift He had, His Son, Jesus Christ. He came to set the captives free and now, I'm free. He has anointed me to set others free. I'm in training for the rest of my life. He has placed a hunger and thirst in my spirit for souls, not only those lost in homosexuality, but all lost souls.

I've been on a press and I'm running to see what the end is going be. During August 2003, I began to attend the church of Pembroke Pines on a regular basis. The most important service I attended was the Saturday and Sunday services. The church was having the TLC (Training, Learning and Caring)

Fair for each one to sign up for Bible study groups they were interested in attending. Well, of course, I signed up for two groups: first, WOW (Women of the Word) and the other group was Breaking Free. Both seemed appropriate.

I always thought of myself to be a woman of the Word and for what I had been freed from just a couple of months before. I was in for the surprise of my life, from both these Bible Studies. When you become serious about God's Business and trust in Him with all your heart, mind, soul, and strength, and acknowledge Him in all things, He will direct your path for "Real." Listen, I've been churched almost all my life; however, the church was not in me. I played church for so many years. I've covered all types of positions in churches: Treasury, Trustee Leaders in prayer and worship team, Counselor of God's people and also deaconess. What a joke!

Now of course, I know what the Bible says about that position. During that time, I had already read the Bible twice, but I was still touching and agreeing with others in the same mess and lifestyle. My Lord began to bring me out and as I remember it took three years. Now reference the TLC Bible classes. It was divine order. Our Lord leads his children "If they desire to be lead." The Holy Spirit directed me to read the book of Esther again while on vacation for two weeks, prior to signing up for WOW, of course. Guess what the first women's study was? Esther! Thank you Lord! That's divine. All the other women we studied in detail. The research gave me new revelation. He who began a good work in me will continue until the day Jesus Christ returns.

There was another Bible class that was a great help in my deliverance: "Breaking Free". These study guides by Beth Moore had me on my knees and in tears of joy and peace to know how much He loves me. My ABBA Father knew exactly what it would take to bring His Prodigal Daughter home.

There is so much more to share and you'll see it in the book to come. All Glory and Praise to the HOLY ONE, God Almighty.

This completes my first revealed testimony.

Chapter 5

I'm a Living Testimony!

There was a struggle after my first testimony. Satan will not let you go easily. I was approached by many brothers and sisters in Christ congratulating me for sharing my testimony so freely. But this one person stood in the corner until the crowd subsided. (God, I pray for myself and other saints for greater discernment and wisdom.) This lady came over and said she was having struggles in the area of lesbianism. She gave me a piece of paper with her phone number and asked me to call her. She said she needed help.

The word of God says in Hosea 4:6 NKJV, *"My people are destroyed for the lack of knowledge."* The

Book of Wisdom says in Proverbs 1:7, *"The fear of the Lord is the beginning of knowledge, but fools despise wisdom and instruction."*

Please listen my sisters and brothers. I personally lacked knowledge and had less wisdom and no discernment and definitely no accountability partner (no person to speak with, with reference to my life encounters.) I've always been one to help others; I just wanted to help. I was wrong as two left shoes. Smile and pray for me. I spoke to her later by phone and invited her to our women's Bible study.

Later, I was involved again in a lustful lesbian affair with this female. I won't get graphic but each time I allowed her to touch me, I became sick after the act was completed. This madness lasted for about six weeks. I cried out for help. I felt so helpless; I disappointed my Jesus. My question in my head was how He can forgive me. Satan was playing with my mind.

I was asked by the director of Bible Study to co-facilitate a women group on "Making Peace with your Past." This was a few weeks after my first testimony. I advised her I would pray for direction. My co-facilitator and I had met each other through other Bible study groups and we are still friends today. I met with Lisa the director of Bible study, to give her a definite no regarding my being a part leader of Bible study. I will explain in detail. I informed Lisa that I had involved myself with another woman in the church for six weeks. I also told her that the involvement was over.

I informed her that I was unworthy of conducting any group, better yet I didn't even know whether I was still saved or not. And yes, I wept and poured out my heart to her after pouring out my heart to the Lord first. I must say what a sweet surrender that was. I was actually submitting myself totally to my Father. Lisa stood in the gap and restored me. Now, you talking about virtuous women, yes, Lisa is a great example of Proverbs 31. With all else on her plate, she shared my burden also and wept with me.

Galatians 6:1 says, *"Brethren, if a man is overtaken in any trespass, you who are spiritual restore such a one in a spirit of gentleness, considering yourself lest you also be tempted."* I thank God for the mature saints walking in the spirit. Now since that time being reconciled, I've been walking in the full fruit of the spirit. Yes, I repent and die daily in order to walk according to the Word. *"Not by might nor by power but by the spirit of the Lord I am able to stand,"* Zechariah 4:6 NIV.

The Affair

Prior to my appointment with Lisa, this diabolical relationship ended seven days before the very morning of my appointment. There were calls from the other party to try and persuade me not to reveal the relationship. This person is a good hearted person, but just was not willing to give up selfish motives and desires. God is seeking those who are willing to be obedient to the cause to serve Him. I was willing to give it all up for his love and comfort; for there is no Greater Love, than Jesus Christ my Lord, Savior and my Redeemer. I'm running on with the Lord; I can't quit.

I partnered with my co-facilitator to teach a 12 week series on "Making Peace With Your Past," for a women's group. The first 12 weeks were in my home on Monday nights from 7-9 p.m. The second 12 weeks were in the Co-facilitator's home back and forth. We were women sharing our hearts and soul. Of course, in all confidentiality it was a must. Each one of us prayed and some cried. I can speak for myself as well as a few others there was much freedom and peace that was beyond my own understanding. The Word of God says *"If I keep my mind on Him, He'll give me perfect peace,"* Isaiah 26:3. I now have it, thanks to our Lord. There is joy, contagious joy, for in his presence there is truly fullness of joy.

Now after six months of "Making Peace with Your Past," we as a group decided to step out to another level. The next session, "Moving Beyond Your Past" was a great 12 weeks of study. Over the course, God was to take greater steps to change our present behavior and attitudes. In this course we were to learn to make new life choices about how we may respond to situations and circumstances rather than simply reacting according to our childhood hurts. This was a great support group. By the time I reached this particular study the exact date was 1/23/06.

The year 2006 was busy for my growth in the Lord, powerful. Where much is given, much is required. I was in love with Jesus and had a true hunger and thirst for Daddy's love and righteousness. All sessions I missed, I made it up on my own. As a group, we studied on recovery - all scripture-based from the Holy Bible. Titles included: Brokenness, Surrender, Cleansing, Honesty, Confessions, Openness, Asking, Intimacy, and Vulnerability. These are the Table of Contents; each chapter once per week was a life support series that was serious. There were many breakthroughs. I thank my Jesus for the Holy Spirit that comforts and teaches.

Chapter 6

Spiritual Preparations

The year 2006 marked a massive search and hunger for the things of God. During March 2006 I attended the School of Ministry Kingdom University, a winter accelerated program of intensive studies. It was taught by the one and only Dr. N. Cindy Trimm. I gained a spectacular wealth of knowledge while witnessing the power of the Holy Spirit. Although the eight courses filled my spirit until my cup runneth over, I was still left with an eagerness for even more knowledge of our Father's household, the Kingdom. I believe Dr. Trimm is an angel in disguise. She is genuine, serious and also humorous. I thank God for allowing her to speak into my life.

Greater Time of Preparation

I believe God was preparing me for greater work on my spiritual journey. In early April 2006 during a week of vacation I arrived at the Georgia Dome in Atlanta to attend Juanita Bynum's "Threshing Floor Revival".

Dr Bynum is a great woman of power given authority by Jesus and the Holy Spirit. I've followed Juanita Bynum's Ministry since the late 90's. She has taught me how to intercede for my family, friends, and myself.

I was not "saved for real" until 2003. But, during this time I was in search of something or someone to complete this vessel. I say to you, try the Son of God, Jesus, and the Holy Spirit. One of my favorite Scriptures, Proverbs 3:5-6, tell us to *"Trust in the Lord with all your heart, and lean not to your own understanding; in all your ways acknowledge him and he will direct your paths."*

My "Threshing Floor Experience" raised my spirit, soul, and my entire being to another level. I couldn't keep it to myself. I was sharing, caring, and praying for others, my family members, friends, and co-workers. Even bringing others to Jesus Christ became and still is such an urgent matter.

We are approaching the end of this age. Time is drawing near. If we love God's people, we must truly have a hunger and thirst to draw others from darkness into the marvelous light. Next level, more devils. I agree with the Word, *"No weapon formed against me shall prosper"*, Isaiah 54:17. This is my heritage as one of God's servants. Yes, he says they will be formed; however, they will not profit anything. Understand that. Remember, in all your getting, receive understanding.

My Continual Preparation in 2006

During my month's vacation, I was in Atlanta GA at the Georgia Dome for MegaFest 2006 with T.D Jakes Ministries. I'm proud to say I partner with T.D Jakes (Aaron's Army), a powerful giant in Christ Jesus. He is a known gift to the body of Christians gifted in many aspects in the Ministries of helps, speaking, teaching, giving caring, and building and much more than I'm qualified to expand on. I share with this reading audience that I have gleaned from TD Jakes Ministry and have been filled to the brim by each encountered experience. All my experience from His Woman Thou Art Loosed Conference, all

Mega Fest Conferences as well as his daily TBN teachings helped me grow spiritually. It's my desire to become an honorable vessel for the Kingdom of God. For at the end of this earthly vessel when I see my Lord face to face, I also desire to hear the Voice of God say "Well done my good and faithful servant. Enter into the kingdom."

Time of Preparation

Each one of us has a friend or two we hang out with that we trust with our heart to tell us the truth even if it hurts. During this period of my spiritual growth, each span of growth for the year of 2006 my friend and I had made plans to attend the Accelerated Class with Dr. Trim and Women on the Frontline in Atlanta. At Mega Fest 2006, my friend had begun a new job and was not able to attend. Well, I viewed this time as God wanting me to rely solely on Him, regardless of who shows up or not. I knew the Lord was with me each step of the way. I stepped out on faith and hope knowing that there was something new brewing in my Spirit.

I was coming in alignment and focus on the things of God. My flesh was beginning to die daily. So I may live, move, and have my being in my Lord.

This experience also took me to another level of my dependency upon the Lord.

My Master's Degree

I yearned to complete my Master's Degree since I received my Bachelor's Degree in 1980. Late August 2006 I completed all paper work, application, transcripts and paid for my class at Trinity University. Now I'm studying for my Master Degree of Arts in religion. I started my study late August '06 and resigned from school October 11, 2006.

My mother took a bad fall and injured her left collar bone (strong side). This meant she had to attend therapy three times a week per the doctor's instructions to gain strength back in her arm. I would take her early enough on Mondays to give me ample time to get her situated with food and run other errands for her. One of her favorites was the dollar store. (Word to the wise brothers/sisters: Honor and cherish and respect your parents while they're on this earth; including you grandchildren and great-grandchildren). I'm not saying let them drain you of all your strength, but learn to love them like you love yourself; stop being selfish. And I'm not boasting.

Every other Monday I gave my time to my mother to attend her personal business and household needs. God gave me plenty of grace, mercy, and wisdom in dealing with my mom's situation. My last dinner with my mother was Sunday, December 3, 2006. Each Sunday I would leave church and check on mother to see if she had been picked up for dinner. On this particular Sunday, I found the house empty. Silence; no one was at home. I was prompted by the Holy Spirit to pray throughout the house. This was something I did on a regular basis. The Spirit of the Lord had me to go in silently and pray through out the house on many occasions when they were asleep and leave as quietly as I had arrived. But this Sunday seemed to have been urgent. Of course, I complied.

After my mother had fallen, she stopped sleeping in her bed and started sleeping in her recliner which was as comfortable as a bed. In the den area near the front door she watched and saw everything that came and went in the neighborhood and in the evening she and her elderly neighbor would sit and talk for hours on the front porch. This was one of her enjoyments.

I prayed the last prayer for this house. I anointed every window, door, and doorknob. When

I entered the den where my mother slept, I accidentally tripped over my mom's chair and spilled the remaining of the anointing oil in her chair. I had to wipe the entire chair as if I was anointing her. On this Sunday soon after I finished anointing the house and praying, my number one niece arrived with my mother after church. My mother was in her Usher Board uniform. She stated she had a great time in service.

I saw that she was in good spirit. I said to her "I'm leaving now that you're ok." She became very demanding, nothing unusual for mom. But there appeared to be an urgency in her voice.

"You're not going anywhere."

"Mom, what do you need?"

My mom is always concerned about everyone else's nutritional needs, mostly her adult children. She asked if I would go and purchase dinner from KFC. And of course, I did. I served her dinner at the table. I sat and ate dinner with her, and we discussed our church services.

Mother was still attending services at Greater New Macedonia Missionary Baptist Church where she served as an usher faithfully for over 33 years. I try not to miss a day checking on my mother by a phone call or just dropping in by the house in route to work or returning to my own house.

On Thursday I was called to the hospital by my mom's neighbor. She called my cell phone at work. I saw three missed calls. I called and she informed me that the ambulance had taken my mom to the hospital. This was mom's last ride by ambulance.

I arrived approximately an hour after she reached the emergency room. As I was approaching the room, the doctor approached me standing face to face just inches away from room 19 and said, "We tried everything; she didn't make it." Immediately I turned from him and looked up toward heaven, threw my hands up and thanked God for receiving her in his arms. I was crying, yet rejoicing, thanking my Lord and Savior for greater peace and joy; her life had just begun anew. On December 7, 2006 early Thursday morning, mother went home to be with the Lord.

Yes, Lord, only you know how much I miss my mom. But when I think about her bringing joy and laughter and remembering the good times we had together tears also come because I miss her presence. And yes, I know she's having a glorious time in heavenly places with you, Lord.

We had some good times and some bad times. But I can tell you the good surely outweighed the bad. And yes, I questioned the Lord. I asked him was he preparing me the early part of this year for my mother's death. Yes, I was upset for a short period of time. I had been studying the Word more intensely and I knew the Lord knows it all.

He is the beginning and the end; he is the alpha and the omega, the first and the last. Also, he is the author and finisher of my faith. I had begun to trust Him totally with my total being and apparently that was just the beginning of what was to come.

Chapter 7

Revised Testimony

I was invited to a women's conference late 2005 to give my testimony. The theme was "Women Redeemed - The Curse Is Broken." I rewrote my testimony according to the theme. But, of course the message still remained the same. I've been delivered, healed, and set free by the Almighty God.

I read and then spoke: "Greetings in the name of Jesus, to each of you. My name is Tonya Lee and I come to speak to you today. I do not come to deliver an eloquent speech. But, I come to share with you God's amazing grace that has been manifested in my life.

I am currently employed as a Corrections Officer. I have made this my career for nearly 21 year. I'm an expert at releasing inmates from jail who are eligible to be released. However, little did I know that my God had placed me in this profession to be healed, delivered, and set free from a lifestyle of homosexuality.

Satan had me bound with the stronghold of lesbianism for 23 years. But to God be the glory, He had the best plans for me. He had his son, Jesus Christ who came to set the captives free. Now he has anointed me to set others free.

I'm in training for the remainder my life. He has placed a hunger and thirst in my spirit for souls. This hunger and thirst is not just for those lost in the spirit of perversion- homosexuality, but all souls that are in bondage.

Now I'm running to see what the end is going to be. I explained to the audience since my deliverance in early 2003 that I've had some trials, tribulations, some temptations and some tests. My choice to walk with Christ has not made me perfect yet. At the present time, I may have not passed every test, but I can say I'm firmly standing with Jesus. Day by day I stand decreeing and declaring the Word of God in

Jesus' name and by the power of the mighty blood of Jesus."

My 1st experience at N.B.L.C.C

The night I opened the door to enter, the door person was quite friendly. I was early as usual. I've always made it my business to be early everywhere I go. I do believe there are greater benefits for one to arrive early in all aspects of life regardless of the occasion. I believe this gives one the opportunity to have the upper hand.

My spirit was at ease in this place of worship. Pastor Ann approached me with a smile, hugged and kissed me while introducing herself at the same time. I felt at home now. We exchanged greetings and pleasures. It was a small congregation; each one that I met was friendly and loving. Wow! What a characteristic of Christ. I felt special; a sweet aroma was in the service.

I was invited to a prayer breakfast the following Saturday. I was very much impressed with the outcome. All the females were dressed in green but me. I didn't get the memo informing me of the dress code, nevertheless, I was still comfortable among my sisters. This prayer breakfast was powerful from the beginning to the end, from the Word spoken to the prayers led by the Pastor.

I was amazed how the Holy Spirit showed up so powerfully in that place of worship at that hotel. The women's conference was over. I returned to my regular church and continued my service and Bible studies at the church of Pembroke Pines. The Women's Group has ended and we were on our holiday break.

I began to visit every other Sunday at New Beginning Life Christian Center (N.B.L.C.C,). I would attend the 8:00 am service at my church and the 11:00 am service at N.B.L.C.C. After about two months, I felt a pull by the Holy Spirit to return to N.B.L.C.C. My friend and I entered the church together and sat in the back. I was called up by the pastor and she immediately began to speak to my spirit. I fell under the power of the Holy Spirit. I left that evening from N.B.L.C.C. feeling free, also knowing somehow by the Spirit that this was where I belonged.

I continued to attend church at N.B.L.C.C every other week for about two months. In March 2006, I began attending weekly. I prayed about it and made a move to cancel my membership at the church of Pembroke Pines on April 28, 2006. I also gave up my appointed position as co-facilitator of the women's group.

While following protocol, I thanked the presiding pastor in letter form for allowing me to be part of the ministry. Yet, it was time for me to move on to further my spiritual growth and development. First and foremost, I thank our Father for his direction to the church of Pembroke Pines which led me to a place where I became "saved for real."

Greater Spiritual Growth and Development

I officially joined membership with N.B.L.C.C on May 7, 2006. My statement to the pastors and the congregation was "I came to be one of the best servants they ever had". Only God knew where He was taking me. I know I was called to be a servant unto the Lord. It's my desire to please my Father in Heaven because I want His will to be my will.

I know He's the only source that has and continues to sustain me and all my doings. It's all for His glory, His great pleasure and even for my good. Sorry! I went off to a little praise. But remember this always, we were born to worship Him in all things, including ways, deeds, and actions. God inhabits the praises of his people.

There is a great anointing in this place. My new spiritual parents ask me to become a part of a new ministry that has been on their hearts for years. Once they asked me, I was determined to be obedient. I researched and found information on the subject of singles ministry. I presented the layout to the Shepherds of N.B.L.C.C. They were surprised, but excited. I was asked to lead this singles group. What a task. "Help Lord." The Lord did indeed help me; we are still in operation.

My ordination

On May 20, 2007, I was ordained as an Associate Minister at New Beginning Life Christian Center under the leadership of Senior Pastor Victor C. Foster and Co-Pastor Ann G. Foster. Wow! Talk about greater work. Where much is given, much is required.

This position has given me more responsibility to be a greater servant. My accountability partner is closer to me than my brother or shall I say my sister. My pastor Ann is my accountability partner and I do believe she tracks me by the Spirit. Those eyes ain't big for nothing. Smile! Let me explain. On many occasions when I was experiencing some form of spiritual, emotional, or warfare trauma she would call with comforting words of wisdom, prayer, or simply directions.

We all need accountability partners. I feel doubly blessed because I'm covered spiritually by having two dynamic pastors who are real and transparent. They both have come through many obstacles in life and are not ashamed to care enough to share, in order to pull other souls out of the darkness and draw them into the marvelous light of the Kingdom of God. This may be through preaching, teaching, evangelism or laying on of Hands.

I often thank God for them as I pray each morning interceding and standing in the gap for them. I decree and declare God's promises over their lives as well as their entire household of the church. And I do believe God is faithful in all His promises to his children. Yes! Amen!

Chapter 8

The Great I Am- He is the Love of my Life

The great "I Am" is the only source; everything else is only resources! Without the Great I Am we are absolutely nothing. I don't care how much you have been told by the world system, you're nothing without Him; but with Him, all things are possible. Because He is the "I Am"

I proclaim that I am a child of God made in the image and likeness of God. I am a child of the Covenant (promise); I'm redeemed from the hand of the enemy. I'm forgiven, saved by grace (for real) through faith. I'm justified and sanctified. Hallelujah! I'm a new creature. I've been crucified with Christ. I am a partaker of His divine nature. I have been redeemed from the powers of darkness, now led by the spirit of God. I'm a child of God being kept in safety wherever I go.

Yes! I'm getting all my needs met by Jesus; I am casting all my cares on Him. Because of the Great I Am, I'm strong in the Lord and in the power of his might. Yes, I'm doing all things through Christ who strengthens me. I'm an heir of God and a joint heir with Jesus. I'm observing and doing the Lord's Commandments.

Yes! Yes! Yes! I'm surely blessed coming in and going out. I am an inheritor of eternal life and I'm blessed with all spiritual blessing. Surely, I'm healed by his stripes. I also am exercising my authority over the enemy.

I am above only and not beneath. Remember who I am; now you too, can make up your mind and get back what the enemy (devil) stole from you. We are more than conquerors, in Christ Jesus. The Great I Am gives us the rights on Earth; for I am an over comer by the Blood of the Lamb and the Word of my testimony. I will not be moved by what I see.

Jesus Christ has given me power and authority of casting down every vain imagination. Daily I am being transformed by a renewed mind; every morning there's new mercies that reign. Again, because of the Great I Am, I am a laborer together with God. I'm the righteousness of God in Christ. I'm surely an imitator of Christ and the Light of the World. I proclaim the Glory of the Lord is around me and I am in the Power of the Spirit and the Spirit of the Lord is upon me.

I have personally received these blessings and promises from the Almighty, the Great I Am. Each one of you who has read this also has the right to receive these gifts and promises for yourself. These blessings are also for your children, friends, neighbors, and co-workers. These gifts are our inheritance.

Always remember the words in Psalm 24:1 NKJV. *"The Earth is the Lord's and all its fullness, the world and those who dwell therein".* Receive Christ now and claim your inheritance today. Once you truly repent and receive Christ as Lord of your life, these are greater blessings and greater works to be completed for the Great Kingdom of Heaven.

There is much more peace when we can lay our selfishness down at the foot of the Cross of Jesus and present our temple as a living sacrifice holy and acceptable unto Him and become His representative here on Earth. Remember the earth and everything in it belongs to God. I don't care how you may stack it or compare to all you think you are or all you were told that you are. It cannot compare to what the Holy Bible says. Choose this day whom you are going to serve. As for me and my house, I'm going to serve the Lord, Joshua 24:15 NJKV. I personally want to be "saved for real".

BEFORE CHRIST

AFTER CHRIST

Greater Testimony-Rewritten Again

For Women's Conference 2006 "Women in the Kingdom-Saved For Real"

Behold He makes all things become new. Greetings in the name of our Gracious Lord and Sovereign Savior! I ask you (again) to read this testimony and journey with me through a supernatural surgery and total transformation that took place in my life. From 23 years of diabolical disobedience and the slow destruction of self into a woman of destiny, declared by the anointed power of the Holy Ghost.

The "before and after" pictures you see are not trick photos with weave and expensive make up applied by back stage professionals. What you are looking at is a real makeover done by the Master's Hands. He is a Keeper and restores me each morning. So, I bodily proclaim that yes, "I am Saved For Real."

Like some church folks, I had become a "pew sitting" devil most of my life. I was a faithful Sunday morning Christian, sung the songs, and danced the dance. I went to the altar repeatedly. I cried, hollered, and even fell out on the floor, but never did I experience true deliverance.

During these fabricated years of being a saint, hearing the Word, but not doing as the Word says and even after reading the Bible twice, I still continued to purse and be bound by my worldly life choices. Like Lot, I was determined to remain in Sodom.

I thank God for His thoughts and ways being much greater than mine. Oh, I didn't tell you or did I? Homosexuality, fueled by the spirit of perversion, was the devil of assassination. The demon's name was Lesbian. Starting at age 23, I dated her faithfully throughout my early 20's, my 30's, and even up to my mid 40's. Instead of the engrafted Word of God bringing about a change, I became very comfortable with a church that accepted me as I was. I took on titles and held many positions of leadership, from deaconess to church trustee, from church treasurer to counselor. What a joke. I also joined the prayer and worship team.

By the way, this particular church was an open door for the gay agenda; a church which stamped an approval for self-righteousness. Although this wicked imprint would last for years on end, God had the original blueprint for "soul prints" plans, all along.

In April 2003, prior to Easter I was led to attend the church of Pembroke Pines on a regular basis. The most important service I've embarked on was a two day "TLC" (Teaching, Learning, and Caring) fair, where each member or attendee had a chance to register and sign up for Biblical studies. Well of course, I registered twice and from those upfront and personal encounters and studies, I boldly became serious about God's business.

I began to see clearly my wrong and fully understood the conviction involved. I became hungry and thirsty for righteousness. I can testify that with my whole heart I'm delivered and now I'm saved, sanctified and fully engulfed in the Holy Spirit. I'm truly *saved for real.*

I do believe He has given me this opportunity to write this book and share my miraculous transformation. I have shared my story for His glory, for my good and for others to be made whole. I praise Him for my change; for God truly inhabits the praises of His people.

I worship Him just because of who He is in my life. What about you? After reading this segment of this book you should have an idea as to who you are by now. If you wish to proclaim his name, receive Him into your life completely, just repent of all your sins and ask for forgiveness. You can get to know Him through His Word which gives true life. He is a giver. Remember John 3:16. He loves you. His Word says, You have not because you have not asked, seek Him and you shall find Him.

Surrender it all. He wants to renew you completely as well. Our Father is in the business of restoring and reviving our lives. He gives new beginnings. He resurrected my life. If he did it for me, he'll do it for you also. Surrender your complete heart. Only He can mold you and make you complete.

Chapter 9

Lost Sheep

I lived a lifestyle of perversion for 23 years; what a state of mind. Now I focus on one of my favorite Psalms I learned as a young girl. I didn't know then but I have learned some mysteries and revelation knowledge of Psalm 23. Our Lord knows how to use what the enemy meant for evil and turn it around for our good.

Let us make it clear for you, the reading audience. Let us review Psalm 23 (NKJV). *"The Lord is my shepherd; I shall not want he make me to lie down in green pastures; He leadeth me beside* the still waters. He restoreth my soul; He leadeth me in the paths of righteousness for His name's sake. Yea though I walk through the valley of the shadow of death, I will fear no evil; for thou art with me, thy rod and they staff they comfort me. You prepare a table before me in the presence of my enemies; You anoint my head with oil; my cup runs over. Surely goodness and mercy shall follow me all the days of my life; and I will dwell in the house of the Lord forever."

Let us share and receive greater revelation, knowledge and understanding of Psalm 23. First, let us research the meaning of the number 23, biblically. Twenty-three: the Lord is my shepherd, I shall not want. The number twenty-three doesn't occur that often in the Holy Bible; when it does, it points to prosperity and plenty. The prosperity can be in a physical, financial or spiritual sense.

The positional aspect of twenty-three is also important. For example, the twenty-third verse in Genesis completes the fifth day of creation when God says to creatures of the earth "Be fruitful and multiply." Note - this does not mean have plenty babies, it's much deeper!

The most familiar "twenty-third" in the Bible is Psalm 23 which definitely speaks of prosperity based on God's provisions. From the beginning of Psalm 23 to the end, we are assured that we shall not want because we have everything we need. We are promised green pastures, still waters, the restoration of our soul; a path of righteousness, a table of abundance in the presence of our enemies a head anointed with oil, a cup that runneth over, goodness and mercy and a dwelling place in the house of the Lord all because of God's grace and His love for us. WOW, WOW, WOW!!! Are you getting this?

When you look at David's Shepherd of Psalm 23 and welcome him as your own shepherd, you can say like David, *"The Lord is my shepherd, I shall not want."*

Now, let's search for even greater knowledge and receiving our Lord as our Shepherd. Question: What is a shepherd? I'm glad you asked. I will attempt to explain. A shepherd is a person who takes care of sheep. Figuratively, the Old Testament pictures God as Israel's Shepherd. Psalm 80:1 states: *Give ear, O Shepherd of Israel, You who lead Joseph like a flock; You who dwell between the cherubim, shine forth!* The New Testament reveals Jesus as the Good Shepherd who gave His life for his sheep.

The sons of Abraham, Isaac and Jacob, herded sheep. Rachel was a shepherdess. David, Moses, and Amos found herding to be excellent preparation for future leadership roles.

Jesus' life exemplifies these leadership traits. Jesus knows each of His sheep intimately. (John 10:3-5) Each sheep knows its shepherd's voice and responds immediately. Even in a large flock, one individual sheep will run to its shepherd when its own name is called. *"My sheep hear my voice and I know them and they follow me."* (John 10:27)

I am the sheep: I declare that the Lord is my Shepherd. I decree it in the name of Jesus. Sheep are curious, but dumb animals, often unable to find their way home even if the shepherd is within sight. According to Psalm 32:8, The Lord says, *"I will instruct you and teach you in the way you should go; I will guide you with My eye ".* Thank you Lord; the shepherd never takes his eyes off wandering sheep.

Often sheep will wander into a briar patch or fall over a cliff in the rugged Palestinian Hills. This is a true picture of the human race. The shepherds tenderly search for their sheep and carry them to safety. And when he comes home, he calls together his friends and neighbors, saying to them, Rejoice with me, for I have found my sheep which was lost. Luke 15:6

I thank God for His appointed and anointed shepherds of the day whom He has assigned to our churches today. The presence of the Shepherd offers comfort to the flock. Our pastors are our spiritual parents.

All Christians are comforted by the presence of the Lord. It is especially comforting when darkness over shadows the believers.

Jesus is our Door; nothing can touch our lives without touching Him first. This is a perfect picture of shepherds, who literally, become the living door of the sheepfold. Shepherds curl up in the door or in the entrance of a cave; they put their bodies between the sleeping sheep and the ravenous animals or thieves. John 10:29 states: *"My Father, who has given them to me, is greater than all; and no one is able to snatch them out of my Father's hands"*. Isn't it wonderful that no one can take us out of the hands of Jesus.

One great day Jesus the Chief Shepherd will return, gather His whole flock into one fold and divide the sheep from the goats. Until that time, Jesus continues His search for every lost sheep. Thank you Jesus for your searching - I once was lost and now I'm found, was blind, now I can see. His sheep are to yield themselves to Him for His useful service until at last, they will dwell in the House of the Lord forever.

My invitation to you is: Come and join the sheepfold, Please!

Repeat this prayer: "Lord, I repent of all my sins, iniquities and transgressions. I ask for your forgiveness. I cast all my cares, my doubts, my worries, my fears, my unbeliefs, my everything. I give them all to you. I thank you Lord for hearing me and forgiving me. Mold me, make me brand new, my mind, my heart, my spirit, soul and body. I give it all to you. What You did for this writer, I believe you can do it for me. In Jesus name I pray, Amen".

God shows no partiality. Salvation belongs to every living creature It doesn't matter what you've done, how long you did it, or who you did it with. Age is not a problem; come and receive your blessing. Welcome home my brother or my sister. I'm now saved for real.

Sign _____

Date_____

Saved for Real Birth Day (spiritual)[3]

Final Acknowledgement of Psalm 23

He also anoints our heads with oil. Shepherds anoint the heads of their sheep to soothe the scratches and wounds. For priests, the anointing oil speaks of consecration to their work. Every believer is anointed with the Holy Spirit the moment he/she receives the Savior. The anointing guarantees us the teaching ministry of the Holy Spirit, we should burst forth with the grateful acknowledgement, "My cup runs over and over and over again".

His love has no limits.

His grace has no measure.

His power has no boundary,

Known to men:

For out of His infinite Riches

In Jesus

He giveth, and giveth and giveth

And giveth again. AMEN! [3]

Chapter 10

Bonds/ Bondages/ Generational Curses

My sisters, my brothers, we will never understand where we are going, until we understand where we are. Also, we need to continue on the path and journey of our deliverance and healing. Now, let us learn and receive knowledge on Bonds, Bondages, Curses, and Generational Curses. First, let us acknowledge that knowledge is power and that power is knowledge. Little knowledge is little power.

What is a Bond?

Based on Webster's Encyclopedic Dictionary of the English Language, a bond is something that binds, fastens, confines, or holds together. Let's look at bonds from the spiritual stand point. According to Nelson's New Illustrated Bible Dictionary, a bond is an obligation or restraint of any kind.

In the Bible, the word is used literally, of the fetters and chains of prisoners (Judges 15:14). In a figurative sense, it refers to the bonds of sin and wickedness (Isaiah 58:6), covenant obligation (Ezek. 20:37), and peace and love (Eph. 4:3). I just want to make it clear that there are two different types of bonds; good or bad. Hopefully, we will choose to link ourselves to the good bonds. There are many bonds, however I will name only a few to clarify my point.

Good Bonds:

    A. Covenant with Christ (salvation is free)

    B. The Church (Partner with the body of Christ)

    C. Pastors- Your Spiritual Parents (Covering)

    D. God's Word (Psalms 119:105) is the Greatest Bond

Bad Bonds

   A. Fornication

   B. Malice

   C. Gossip

   D. Murder

Webster's Dictionary states that bondages are slavery or involuntary servitude; serfdom. Bondages are also the state of being bound by or subjected to some external power or control.

As we search for the answer to bondage it's noted that it is the same as being in slavery. What does it mean to be in slavery? My sister, my brother, let us lean more together. The Bible contains warning about the practice of slavery. The Old Testament prophet, Amos, spoke woe to Gaza for their practices of slave-trading entire populations (Amos 1:6-9). The Book of Revelations declares that disaster awaits those who sell slaves (Rev. 18:13). As for Christians, the Apostle Paul advised slaves to obey their master: Bondservants, be obedient to those who are your masters according to the flesh, with fear and trembling, in sincerity of heart, as to Christ. Eph. 6:5.

Both slave and free are called upon to receive the gospel of Jesus Christ. In Christ, social distinctions such as slavery no longer apply: *Where is neither Greek nor Jew, circumcised nor uncircumcised, barbarian, Scythian, slave nor free, but Christ is all and in all.* Col. 3:11.

In Christ, we are all brothers and sisters. The excitement of such new relationship is expressed by Paul: *"Therefore you are no longer a slave but a son, and if a son, then an heir of God through Christ".* Gal. 4:7

In a spiritual sense, people apart from Christ are slaves to sin. John 8:34 tells us that whoever commits sin is a slave of sin. When we are free from sin, we become slaves of righteousness. Christ can set us free from this kind of slavery.

Paul spoke of himself as a "servant", a word sometimes rendered as "bondservant" but frequently also as a "slave" (Romans 1:1, Titus 1:1) Christians, especially ministers, are not hired servants, but slaves committed to service to Jesus. Slaves do not manage their own lives. People who call themselves slaves of Christ acknowledge that the Savior has power over them.[4] Amen, I touch and agree.

I became a Christian and a Minister of the Gospel; I agree with Apostle Paul one hundred percent. I have surrendered my entire being unto the Lord which includes my whole spirit, soul, and body so He may use this temple for His glory. I boast only of my weaknesses.

I'm A Christian

When I say I am a Christian, I'm shouting I was saved by His grace and mercy. I'm whispering I was lost, that's why I chose His Way.

When I say I am a Christian, I don't speak of this with pride. I confess that I still struggle needing God to be my guide.

When I say I am a Christian I'm not trying to be strong. I'm professing that I'm weak and pray for strength to carry on.

When I say I am a Christian I'm not bragging of success. I'm admitting I have failed and can never pay the debt.

When I say I am a Christian I don't think I know it all. I submit to my confusion asking humbly to be taught.

When I say I am a Christian, I'm not claiming to be perfect. My flaws are all too visible but God believes I'm worth it.

When I say I am a Christian, I still feel the sting

of pain. I've had my share of heartaches, that's why I seek his face.

When I say I'm a Christian, I do not wish to judge. I have no authority; I only know I am loved by Him.

-Anonymous

Let us continue on in acknowledgement of curses as I mentioned in the first part of this chapter. First of all, we as God's created people have the right to choose curses or blessing upon our life. We will discuss curses and give the reading audience a measure of understanding on generational inheritance curses. Not a one of us is exempt.

Biblically, what is a curse? It is a prayer of injury, harm, or misfortune to befall someone. Noah, for instance, pronounced a curse on anyone who cursed Canaan (Genesis 9:25). Isaac pronounced a curse on anyone who cursed Jacob (27:29). The soothsayer Balaam was hired by Balak, King of Moab, to pronounce a curse on the Israelites (Numbers 22-24). Goliath, the philistine Giant of Gath, "cursed David by his God" (I Samuel 17:43) .

In Biblical times, a curse was considered to be more than a mere wish that evil would befall one's enemies; it was believed to possess the power to bring about the evil the curse spoke. In the New Testament, Jesus cursed the fig tree saying, "Let no fruit grow on you ever again," and immediately the fig tree withered away (Matthew 21:19, Mark 11:14). Jesus also taught Christians how to deal with curses. "Bless those who curse you." (Luke 6:28)

The Apostle Paul spoke of the law as a curse because it pronounces a curse upon everyone who does not continue in all things which are written in the Book of the Law. (Galatians 3:10) By the grace of God, however, Christ has redeemed us from the curse of the Law, having become a curse for us (for it is written, cursed is everyone who hangs on a tree) Gal 3:13. John promised that the day is coming when "there shall be no more curses" (Rev 22:3). All those whose names are written in the Lamb's Book of Life will enjoy the abundant blessings of God. [5]

Now! Let us also discuss spirits of inheritance/generational curses. Again I say to you, more knowledge equals more power. Receive your blessings of understanding and wisdom for wisdom is a principal thing. [5]

Biologists, sociologists, and psychologists all agree that there lies within man propensity for certain idiosyncratic behaviors, tendencies, traits, weaknesses, strengths, and habits peculiar to particular families. They say these things are passed down by the programming of the DNA.

According to Exodus 20:5 God says, *"I the Lord thy God am a jealous God unsetting the inquiry of the fathers upon the children unto the third and fourth generation..."* This Scripture let's us know that we are dealing with intergenerational Spirits, which are responsible for producing the following:

- Family- Community Peculiarities
- Ancestral Eccentricities
- Idiosyncrasies
- Ethnic traits
- Social Tendencies
- Clannish Oddities
- Pathological Conditions of the Mind and Body
- Individualities
- Fundamental Values
- Cultures
- Passions
- Motives
- Indignations
- Agendas
- Habits
- Ideologists

- Perceptions
- Temperaments
- Personalities
- Illnesses
- Degenerative Diseases
- Congenital Diseases
- Eventualities (Things that lie dormant and go undetected for years)

To those individuals who desire to improve their spiritual growth and situations and or circumstances, I recommend reading materials that will increase your knowledge and help you gain spirituality. I'm personally speaking directly to the reader who cares to enlarge, renew, restore their territory (life). The most important advice I can give you is: Invest in yourself.

Remember the Word says in all your getting, get also understanding. (I Thess. 5:23-25 NIV) *"May God Himself, the God of Peace, sanctify you through and through. May your whole spirit, soul, and body be kept blameless at the coming of our Lord Jesus Christ".* The one who calls you is faithful and he will do it.

I am recommending ten books that I have read. That's just a start. There are many others and yes,

I've read all I'm recommending; reading is my hobby. But don't neglect reading the most important Book of all books while reading the list of books. I highly recommend the oldest book ever written, yet the Author is still alive - The Holy Bible, God's Word. Please! Read daily.

The list of books including in the references at the end of this book are only the beginning of your new journey. And for those individuals who are dealing with spirits of perversions or any other bondage or strongholds, I recommend *"101 Satanic Weapons Used Against the Saints"* by Dr. Cindy Trim. This book will give you great insight as how to combat the enemy's weapons. Remember, more knowledge equals more power.

God Himself has given us the power and authority to take back what rightfully belongs to us.

He says it in His Word and His Word has been established in Heaven forever. God says to take dominion, replenish. Genesis 1:28

Renew your mind daily. Stop conforming to the way of this world, but be transformed by the renewing of your mind. Romans 12:1-2. Let us stop giving into fear of the enemy and let's begin to turn the table around on the enemy. We will fear the Lord, only. Obey and respect Him in all that He says in the Word. It's time to put the enemy under our feet where he belongs and keep him there. Let us now MAGNIFY the Lord together. He's worthy.

I've come to the end of this chapter. I'm hoping you have gained within, some form of knowledge and not just head knowledge. I'm hoping your heart has made a transformation.

If you have read this book with an open heart, I'm sure there are many questions unanswered either for yourself or friend or family members. The next and final chapter will be question and answers.

Now, I don't claim to be an expert in this field. I'm answering all these questions according to my past 23 years of living in that lifestyle. As a former lesbian, I'm hoping to help answer to the best of my knowledge and with the help of the Holy Spirit, who's my Teacher and Comforter. He's the wind beneath my wings and the fire in my soul for my soul thirsts for Him each morning, noon, and night.

Yes, I'm on a journey upward. However, I will receive many blessings while I'm still here on this Earth. I'm waiting for Jesus' return. While I wait, I ask in Jesus' Name that He continue to direct my path. I ask that my Lord continue to keep a hedge of protection around those I love and hold so dear to my heart. And please, Lord, keep me.

Again I pray one of my favorite Scripture, I Thessalonians 5:23-24 NKJV. *"Now may the God of Peace Himself sanctify you completely; and may your whole Spirit, soul, and body be preserved blamelessly at the coming of our Lord Jesus Christ. He who calls you is faithful, who also will do it."* For you and I believe and trust Him our Lord to turn it around for you. There are new mercies each morning. Amen! So be it.

If you believe, sign below.

Sign Here _____

Welcome Home and receive the Kingdom Blessings.

Chapter 11

Questions and Answers

I t's my desire to hopefully bring some form of clarity to many of the readers of this book, "Saved for Real". I know I will not be able to satisfy everyone's curiosity but hopefully bring some clarity and understanding to many. Remember, with the help of the Holy Spirit, I'm answering these questions from my own experiences of 23 years of my involvement in this diabolical Spirit of Perversion.

Many of the questions come from friends and others who have family members involved in the lifestyle of homosexuality or lesbianism and other questions from those who have made a conscious decision to be set free from the bondage of this Spirit of Perversion.

To answer these questions, I call upon my experience and the existence of the Holy Spirit that dwells within me. I'm praying for souls to be healed, delivered, and set free from bondages of all kind. God is able to do all things but fail.

1. What was your purpose for writing this book?

This book has been written to expose the tactics and strategies of the enemy. This book was written for all of us who have been in bondages and strongholds including: homosexuality, alcohol, drugs, gambling, spirit of madness, and mental illness, spirit of affliction and many others.

Remember, the enemy doesn't like you or me. He came to steal, kill, and destroy. It's time for us to take back what the enemy has stolen, We must bring back to life what he has killed - our dreams, our desires and our hopes. He's destroying our children. It's time for us to turn the table over on Satan and destroy his kingdom. He's a liar, the Father of Darkness, and there is no truth in Him.

We have the power in our tongue. Make the decision now, to fight the good fight of faith. According to, 2 Timothy 2:15, we should *"Be diligent* t*o present yourself approved to God, a worker who does not need to be ashamed, rightly dividing the word of truth."* Choose to know who you are and to whom you belong. Amen!

2. Why are you being so straight forward in your writing?

Smile! Maybe because I'm "straight" now. Lol! There is nothing wrong with a little humor. Well, now I'm saved for real! Or do you mean why am I telling the truth? I know now the whole truth. His Word, His promises, His percepts, are all mine. They have set me free. It is my hope that my testimonies and the blood of the Lamb will set others free from the power of Darkness and bring you and others into the knowledge and power of His marvelous light, the kingdom of Heaven. *Oh, taste and see that the Lord is good. Blessed is the man who trusts in Him! Oh fear the Lord, you His saints! There is no want to those who fear Him.* Psalm 34:8, 9a Amen!

3. Why can't I live my own lifestyle anyway I desire and have a relationship with the Lord and go live in paradise eternally?

First let's stop fooling ourselves. Take off the blinders. We are selfish individuals by nature. We want our cake and ice cream and we want it how we want it. But, if you knew ice cream was laced with poison, would you eat it? I don't think so.

Now, let's look at this question again in this world's system. We have been given privileges and rights. Most of us have contaminated both our privileges and rights by the choices we have made. These poisonous contaminates include touching and agreeing with the things of this world, such as our dysfunctional families, activities, neighborhood gatherings, school systems, our work places and disillusioned relationships.

Many of our choices have not always been proper. We have chosen to rely on our own wisdom. We must become aware that there is only one Source and that's the Mighty and Awesome One. The earth is the Lord's and all its fullness, the world and those who dwell therein.

God wants to renew you, restore you, and revive you for the greater works for the kingdom of God. He requires holiness and sanctification for you. In

His Word, Jesus says repent of your sins, ask for forgiveness, turn from your destructive ways and seek the righteousness of God and all other things will be added unto your life. He is still seeking after your heart.

He's coming back soon! Please choose righteousness.

4. Why do many say that they were born a homosexual individual?

This is absolutely false. Each of us has chosen to live this lifestyle because we are in darkness. I'm speaking to those individuals who have come out or those who want to be freed of this lifestyle.

Please listen. It was good for my flesh when I was involved in lesbian relationships. Yes, I was consumed by my flesh. I was blinded by the lust demons of Satan. I was also lost in my heart and mind. I couldn't see anyone but me, myself, and I. It was all about my own desires. Yes, I've always done good deeds. I helped others that were in need. And I don't doubt you are doing good deeds as well because you are a good person. But doing good deeds will not get you into heaven.

Now, let us go back go back to the beginning of the fall of man. The first Adam fell from God's grace when he chose to eat the forbidden fruit with his wife, Eve. They were both expelled from the Garden of Eden. Sin was upon the Earth from then on.

But thanks to God, He had a back up plan. He sent His only Son, Jesus, upon the Earth (our second Adam) to restore, revive, and take dominion over the land. Everything on it and under it, in the sky and sea, God says it is good. Yes and yes, all this to get a clear answer. He then said now let us (God the Father, God the Son, and God the Holy Spirit) make man in our image and according to the likeness of ourselves. So God created man, He created Him; male and female He created them. God said what He made was very good.

My sisters, my brothers, God has given us all a heart conscience to know when we have gone beyond boundaries. Many are caught up in spirits of pride and rebellions, and no longer have a teachable spirit. Many are in bondage of fear, tactics, and strategies of Satan; many are still stagnated today. It's my way or the highway. I'm praying daily for lost souls to come to the end of themselves so they may be awakened to the only one that can save their souls from the pit of Hell.

We must come to realization and revelation that the entire word of God, The Holy Bible, is absolutely true, not just parts of it. Call on Jesus, the only way, truth, and life. He's waiting for you, now. His arms are still open to receive you. Only He can soften our calloused hearts. It's truly a matter of the heart. It is His will that none will perish. Will you please receive Him today?

This is my prayer for those who are willing to be obedient to God and serve Him. Our "ABBA" Father, I come to you in the name of Jesus and His powerful blood. This prayer of intercession is on the behalf of those who have been blinded and allowed their hearts to be hardened by the enemy's deceptions. In Jesus' name, I bind the hands of Satan upon each one who has been taken captive in their heart and mind, their will, emotions, physical being, and finances. I bind the strongman "Spirit of Perversion" in Jesus name and I loose every sign, system, and manifestation upon these vessels that were created by the most high sovereign God.

Now I release the mind of Christ upon each one who prays this prayer. Open your heart to receive your inheritance from the kingdom of God. I release again the mind of Christ, the Anointed One, the fruit of the Spirit upon you. I release complete healing and full deliverance upon you. Amen!

Now this is not altogether an emotional thing. Just believe and receive what's yours. Begin to die daily of your flesh. Take time to know yourself by spending time with Jesus by reading His Word. Trust Him and believe Him. Allow the Holy Spirit to guide and direct your path. No more searching for love throughout this world. Find Him waiting to embrace you. If you believe by faith, you shall receive Him. Come on in.

Sign Here _____

New Spiritual Birth Date _____

Note: Repent daily of your sins, impurities, and transgressions, your ways, deeds and actions, and your attitudes and behaviors.

5. Why is it that when you finally say 'enough', a thousand things come your way to try and break you down?

Remember, once you said 'yes' to our Savior and Lord, you have renounced Satan's kingdom of darkness. You have accepted the Lord as your Savior and Lord of your life; Satan is angry. But cheer up and remember this always: Satan has no power.

All power and authority has been given to our Savior and Lord. Once Jesus died for all our sin, He went to Hell and bound Satan's powers. He took the keys of power and authority from Satan, and He rose on the third day with all power and authority in His hands. Satan's powers are limited to deceptions only.

He lies and accuses every believer. Don't give Him power over you anymore. You must begin to ask, seek, and knock and continue to ask, seek, and knock. You must keep you mind on the Lord. Only He can give you perfect peace, not your situations or circumstances. Pursue the Lord's presence; you will be strengthened in your weaknesses.

Also, you'll find fullness of joy. Open your heart; he's knocking, ready to fill you with His glory. We as Christians will be tested. It is necessary for us to walk by faith and not by sight. Our eyes will deceive us every time. We are the righteousness of God and many are the afflictions of the righteous but God delivers us from them all.

My sisters, my brothers we are on a journey. There will be trials, tribulations, and many temptations. Just know without a doubt that you are more than a conquer in Jesus Christ. We are over comers by the blood of the Lamb and our testimonies. Never forget, greater is He that is within you than He that is in the world.

6. **Why is it when we don't want to think about other females, or males, alcohol, drugs, gambling, etc. anymore, all these memories rush to our minds?**

The enemy, Satan is very skillful at sending out his every demonic cohorts to watch and seek whom they may devour. The Word says he is like a roaring lion. Good news! He is not a lion. But we are so set to giving him the power as if he is. Satan's deception is limited. Place this deception beneath your feet where it belongs and keep it there.

Stop participating in conversations that are not going to increase your Spirit and Soulish man. The Word of God says for us to work out our soul salvation with fear and trembling. Remember, it is God who works in you both to will and to do His good pleasure. You're now a light bearer. Satan wants to steal, kill, and destroy your witness and testimony because you are no longer his.

Be still and know that our God is still on His throne. He's in charge. You must keep seeking His face and your thirst will be filled. If there is anything in your heart that should not be, lay it at His feet, for God knows even the unknown sins.

Let Jesus mold you, make you, guide and direct you back on a right path. Once you accept Jesus, He transfers power and authority to you. Acknowledge the Word of God. Although we walk in the flesh, we don't war according to the flesh and blood. For the weapons of our warfare are not carnal but mighty through God for pulling down strongholds (satanic influences, lusts of all kind). Cast (pulling) down arguments, Satan's deceptions of anger, malice, gossip, and even disobedience. Cast down arguments and every high thing that exalts itself against the knowledge of God, every principality, bringing every thought into captivity to the obedience to Christ.

Paul, an apostle of Jesus Christ wrote in II Corinthians 4:7-10 NKJV, *"But we have earthen vessels, that the excellence of the power may be of God and not of us. We are hard pressed on every side, yet not crushed. We are perplexed but not in despair, persecuted but not forsaken; struck down but not destroyed. Always carrying about in the body, the dying of the Lord Jesus, that the life of Jesus also may be manifested in our body."* Again I say to you, continue to be strong in the Lord and grow in the Word. The more deposit of God's Word, the more return.

Be blessed.

7. Why is it when we pray for strength, someone comes and brings us back into the same foolishness we just prayed about?

As Christians, we are being tested all day long and each test we pass, we go from faith to faith to glory to glory; from one level to another level. Those of us who wish to be used as a greater servant for the most high God (El Elohim in Hebrew), we must persevere through these tests for perseverance builds hope of glory to a dying world.

The world's system is full of contaminated, unprofitable distractions in which most cases lead to foolishness. Saints, we must understand when Jesus ascended to Heaven and took His seat on the right side of our Father in Heaven, he transferred all powers and authority to every saint. As believers, we must walk away from attacks and storms and all those things that easily beset us.

Webster's Dictionary and Thesaurus defines foolishness as foolish behavior, foolish acts or ideas, nonsense, and silliness. Many people claim to be a child of God but do not walk in faith. God commands that we walk in perfection. He says that He's holy and perfect and He expects us to be holy and perfect (mature) as well.

Many believers are still allowing the world's system to distract them. Some are still caught up in their own flesh. Our spirit man should be so strong and powerful that our body will be subject to our spirit and our spirit subject to our soul. Spending time reading the *"Word"* should be second nature. We should take a dose of spiritual food each morning, evening, and night. The Bible says in I Corinthians 10:13 that He gives us strength to overcome every temptation.

Now, I'm not saying that you have to be in church 7 days a week and 24 hours a day. Many believers today don't care to fellowship with other Christians nor be under a covenant Shepherd. You're being disobedient for the Word of God says, *"Do not forsake the assembly of His house,"* Hebrews 10:25. We all need to be held accountable. This is what your pastors and spiritual parents are for. These are God's assigned shepherds. Wake up my sisters and brothers. Come out of Egypt (Exodus). Many of us Christians are still being influenced by Satan's little elms, because we refuse to surrender and summit our all unto God. Word to the Wise!

Recommendation: Pleases read again the entire book of Proverbs, the great book of wisdom. Also read the book of James in its entirety. Do this for your increase in spirit, soul, and body. Jesus loves you so much! Take time for you. Before reading, pray and ask for wisdom, revelation knowledge, and understanding of the Word of God.

8. Why is it so hard to stop sinning when we know in our hearts that it's wrong?

There are many times we have issues with our flesh because our hearts are wrong. We may still be participating in fleshly deeds, actions and ways. For example we still watch T.V programs that do not fill us with godly spirits. We also involve ourselves in conversations that do not promote Jesus.

Once we are saved by God's grace and make Jesus Christ Lord of all, everything we do should be unto the Lord. We know that sanctification is a process, but it should not take an inordinate amount of time to obtain it.

Each of us should choose to live holy and righteous and present our whole being unto our Lord. Understand this, we are also at war with our flesh and spirit. But remember, the battle is already won. Relax, let go and let God. He's our Jehovah Nissi, our band of victory. He says we are more than a conqueror in Christ Jesus. Continue to hide God's Word in your heart so you may not sin against Him.

Remember, repent of your unfaithfulness, unbelief, and lack of trust. Also remember this, the Holy Spirit gives us power and authority to defeat the enemy. But, we must line up with the principals of the precious Word of God, in order to walk in the promises and blessings He has for His children.

Its time you make a choice to come outside of the belief system of the world system. Begin to seek Him whole heartedly and know you have the power in your mouth and hands. Don't just speak the truth, live the truth. Receive and believe by faith that in God, you are more.

9. Why does it feel like God is not listening to my prayers when I'm asking Him to help me stop fornicating with others, females, males, or both.

It's time to surrender and submit it all to God. The Word of God says submit to him and resist the devil and he will flee from you. Come near to God and He will come near to you (James 4:7-8). We must humble ourselves and ask for help from the

Holy Spirit to strengthen us in our weakness, for we all have weaknesses.

God hears the prayers of all His children. He hears all of those who have sincerely, consciously, heartfully accepted His son as their Savior. We are more than conquerors through Christ Jesus. It is not a feeling; it's a knowing in your spirit that you are victorious over your flesh. You will walk more in the Spirit and not in the flesh as you increase your spirit man. God has given us an offer of life or death.

In Deuteronomy 30:19 NIV it states, *"This day I call Heaven and Earth as witnesses against you that I have set before you life and death, blessings and curses. Now choose life so that you and your children may live."* Satan can only enter in by your invitation. For example, lust of the eyes, lust of the flesh, and pride of life all cause death. I urge you again to choose life.

10. Why is it that when we've made up our mind and want to do the right thing, there's always someone right there to remind us of all the things we've done wrong in the past?

The enemy will always use others that are close to you to accuse you of past sin. It may be close friends, family including mom, dad, sisters, or brothers. He, Satan, is the accuser of the brethren. We've been warned in the Word of God. Satan is the Father of Lies. He's unable to tell the truth.

It is time for us to stay sober and vigilant. Let us focus and ask for daily wisdom and discernment from our Heavenly Father. He gives to each one generously. With these gifts of wisdom and discerning of the spirits, you will be able to know with assurance that certain behaviors are purposed to be of God or of the opposite, satanic maneuver.

Remember again that you've got the power. Now use what Jesus has already given you. We have not, for we have not asked. Make sure you're asking according to His will, purpose, and plan for your life, regardless of what mortal man accuses you of in the past or future. Jesus has already redeemed us by His holy and righteous blood, which was shed in seven places before reaching his final destiny at Calvary. You are covered by the blood. He has died for your sins, every one of them.

"There is now no condemnation to those who are in Christ Jesus because through Christ Jesus, the law of the Spirit of Life, set me free from the law of Sin and Death," Romans 8:1-2. We no longer have to walk according to the flesh, but according to the Spirit. We must stand on the Word of God (our big

daddy), not man. As we get in His presence, there is the fullest of joy. And as we continue to seek His face, He gives us greater peace and understanding. We must learn to let go and let God for He cares about everything that concerns you.

May God continue to bless you with His great and awesome gift of His presence. May our Lord of Peace continue to give you strength to fight the good fight of faith. Jesus loves you so much and so do I! To all my sisters and brothers, *I'm Saved for Real!*

Tonya Lee

Resources and References

Books

Pig in the Parlor, The Practical Guide to Deliverance; Frank and Ida Mae Hammond

Unbroken Curses, Hidden Source of Trouble in the Christian's Life; Rebecca Brown, M.D and Daniel Yoder

He Came to Set the Captives Free; Rebecca Brown, MD

A Divine Revelation of the Spiritual Realm; Mary Baxter

Total Forgiveness; R.T Kendall

The Final Quest; Rick Joyner

Beauty for Ashes Receiving Emotional Healing; Joyce Meyer

Battlefield of the Mind; Joyce Meyer

Believing God; Beth Moore

The Purpose Driven Life; Rick Warren

Nelson's New Illustrated Bible Dictionary

New King James Bible

Memory Verses

Please add the following Scriptures to your reading list for your spiritual growth. All Scriptures are from the New King James Version (NKJV) unless otherwise noted.

Chapter 4
II Corinthians 5:17
Mark 3:5

Chapter 5
Proverbs 1:7
Galatians 6:1
Zechariah 4:6 NIV
Isaiah 26:3

Chapter 6
Proverbs 3:5-6
Isaiah 54:14

Chapter 8
Psalms 24:1
Joshua 24:15
John 3:16
Romans 8:16
Genesis 1:26
Acts 3:25
Psalms 107:2
Colossians 1:13-14
Ephesians 2:8, 6:10
Romans 5:1; 8:17
I Corinthians 6:11
Psalms 91:11
1 Peter 5:7
Revelation 12:11

Chapter 9
Luke 15:6
Psalms 23
Psalms 80:1
John 10:27, 29

Chapter 10
Judges 15:14
Isaiah 58:6
Ezekiel 20:37
Ephesians 4:3
Psalms 119:105
Amos 1:69
Ephesians 6:5
Revelation 18:13
Colossians 3:11
Galatians 4:7

Chapter 11
II Timothy 2:15
Psalms 1,27,37,51,103,
         139,150
II Chronicles 7:14
Isaiah 40:31; 53:5;55:8-9
Matthew 6:33
Proverbs 3:5-6
II Corinthians 4:7-10
Hebrews 10:25
James 4:7-8
Deuteronomy 30:19
Romans 8:1,2

References

[1] "The Rules of Engagement/Binding the Strong Man" by Dr. N. Cindy Trimm, pages 142-144

[2] Nelson's New Illustrated Bible Dictionary, pages 1164 - 1165

[3] Believer's Bible Commentary, Annie Johnson Flint, William Macdonald, Edited by Art Farstad, page 587, paragraph 3 and 4

[4] Nelson's New Illustrated Bible on Slavery, page 39

[5] Binding the Strong Man, Dr. N. Cindy Trimm, pages 54-55

About the Author

TONYA Y. LEE has been in Law Enforcement for 28 years. She is an unsung heroine. As a Juvenile Custody Officer, Tonya has an impact on the rehabilitation of female youthful offenders.

Tonya attained a Bachelor's degree in Social Work from Florida International University and seeks to continue her studies in Theology. She serves as an ordained Associate Minister to Pastors Carnell and Ann Foster of New Beginning Life Christian Center in Hollywood, Florida. She faithfully leads the Saturday morning Prayer and Intercession group, instructs monthly Single's Ministry classes, and also teaches Sunday School on a monthly basis.